BERMUDA ROCK LESSONS

THE Science Project NONSUCH ISLAND

by Ezra Turner

Illustrated by Steven Raynor

Dedication

To my Father, the late

Reginald Leroy "Peter Rabbit" Trott

November 18th, 1930 – December 28th 2008

for his words

"If you move slowly, then move early"

ISBN: 978-1-926609-01-0

Published by Print Link
Printed in Canada

Contents

Acknowledgements

The Author would like to thank

Dr. Judith Hayward

and a special thanks to

Jeremy Madeiros

CHAPTER ONE

The Assignment

Chris Watson was fourteen years old and lived with his parents and twin sisters Carol and Sara in an old Bermuda cottage near the Botanical Gardens.

Chris was a child that always had problems with his school work and had a hard time concentrating on his assignments, taking much longer to finish his school work than the rest of his classmates, who often teased him and called him names. That made him feel dejected and dreading going to school. So much so that he began making up excuses so that he could be excused from school. Tummy aches were his favorite complaint for skipping school.

One morning, after another pretend ailment failed to persuade his father, Chris arrived in class to find Mrs. Burt, his science teacher, looking very pleased. She was usually happy but today she looked positively bubbly. Smiling, she announced a special project. "Class," she said, "I have a project for you that will count for fifty percent of the grade you need to enter high school. Make sure you pay close attention." Turning towards the blackboard, Mrs. Burt wrote in bold, capital letters the word *ENDEMIC*. She then listed various endemic plants and animals introduced to Nonsuch Island by Dr. David Wingate, the now retired Conservation Officer of the Bermuda Government.

Chris gulped at Mrs. Burt's next move. Looking right at Chris she said, "Please stand up and explain the meaning of the word endemic to the class." Chris rose but then lowered his head and said nothing. His classmates began to laugh. Mrs. Burt shushed the class and repeated her question.

"Is it some kind of flu?" Chris asked meekly. At this the class howled to the point of being out of control. Mrs. Burt threatened detention and told Chris to sit back down.

"Okay," she said, "endemic means species that exist nowhere in the world outside of the country or island in which they flourish." Then she delivered the bombshell. "I want you to tell me everything you can find out about the endemic species Dr. Wingate introduced to Nonsuch Island. You have two weeks until exam time and this project will be your homework until then."

Tommy Smith, who was always outspoken in class, quickly raised his hand. "Are you going to show us what these plants and animals look like?" he asked.

"No," Mrs. Burt replied as the whole class sighed in unison. "That is for you to find out. And one more thing," she added, "There will be extra credit for any information you find on other plants and native species introduced to Nonsuch by Dr. Wingate."

"Where are we supposed to look for this information?" Tommy asked.

"You'll find all the information you need to complete the assignment in the library at the Botanical Gardens," Mrs. Burt said.

Harry Minors interrupted her and said, "That's okay for plants but what about animals?"

"Harry, please raise your hand when you wish to speak," Mrs. Burt responded. At that, Harry raised his hand and repeated his question. Now his teacher acknowledged him. "A tour boat goes out to Nonsuch Island once a week. The new Government Conservation Officer, Mr. Madeiros, gives tours of the island. Tell your parents about them. It would make a great family outing."

The whole class began looking around at each other. No one spoke but their glances said it all. How would researching plants and animals possibly make for a fun afternoon or weekend?

ENDEMIC
SPECIES
OF
BERMUDA
HOMEWORK
MATHS
CH.4
PAGE.165

CHAPTER TWO

If You Move Slowly Then Move Early

At the end of the school day Chris braced himself for the ribbing he knew he would get from his classmates on the bus ride home. Sure enough tease him they did, laughing that he thought the word endemic meant flu. Chris was relieved when he finally arrived back home. However, once there he found his mother struggling to amuse the twins and seeming relieved to see him. Looking expectantly at Chris, she asked him to take the twins off her hands while she prepared dinner. Chris protested, "I have an important homework project to do."

"What's the project?" his mother asked.

"I have to research the plants and animals Dr. Wingate introduced to Nonsuch Island."

"Well," said his mother, "that should be easy enough. You have every plant in the Botanical Gardens labeled. Not to mention the library."

"Yes," replied Chris, "but how can I do that with the twins tagging along?"

"Let them help you," offered his mother.

"Good idea," said Chris, as he left her alone to prepare dinner.

When Chris and the twins reached the Gardens, the girls began running around as if they hadn't been outdoors for a year. When they finally tired themselves out, they plopped down under a tree whose sturdy grayish-green leaves fanned up into stiff points. Chris noticed that the tree had a label. "Bermuda Palmetto," he read out loud so that the twins would know the name too. It took them a while to get the pronunciation right but they finally mastered it before mustering the energy to start running around again.

After deciding they'd had enough fresh air, Chris, Carol and Sara returned home to find their father already seated at the table waiting for their mother to serve dinner. As usual, Mrs. Watson told the children to hurry up and wash their hands so dinner could begin. When they were all seated around the table, Mr. Watson performed his customary duty of blessing their food. When he had finished, Sara added, "Thank God for the Bermuda Palmetto." Mrs. Watson smiled at this and informed her husband of Chris's science project on endemic species.

Mr. Watson nodded his head approvingly and said, "That sounds like a fun assignment Chris. Don't forget you can find a lot almost on your doorstep."

Later that night after the dishes were all washed and put away, Mrs. Watson went into the children's room to read them a bedtime story. Afterwards their father came in to kiss them goodnight. The girls were already asleep but Mr. Watson kissed them anyway. As he was leaving the room, he turned to Chris, who was still wide awake, and said, "Son, don't forget your prayers."

"How could I Dad. I need all the help I can get. If I don't pass this science assignment I'm going to be the oldest student in Middle School."

Knowing that his son was usually slow at finishing assignments, Mr.Watson put his hand on Chris' shoulder and said, "The swift don't always win the race."

Chris replied, "That's the way it goes in fairy tales. In real life the swift always come in first."

His father replied, "There's an old saying 'If you move slowly then move early.' As Chris looked confused, his father said, "Son, you have two weeks to learn as much as you can. The sooner you start, the more prepared you'll be." Then he added, "Let me help you." With that Mr. Watson said good night and left the room.

CHAPTER THREE

The Stranger

The next day was Saturday and, as was usually the case on weekends, Chris had no trouble getting up early. However, this Saturday he was on a mission. He had made up his mind to put his father's advice into action. Picking up a pencil and writing pad, Chris walked all the way into town to the library. Once there, he looked around at the books, all neatly lined up on cedar shelves. Actually, the library did not seem that big; just two aisles wide. He chose one aisle and began slowly walking down it, looking for any book marked endemic. However, the only books he saw that seemed remotely useful were ones on Bermuda's coastal areas and the mainland. By the time Chris reached the end of the aisle, he had become a little discouraged. In fact, he had to bite his lip and work up courage to go to the next aisle. But determined, he made the effort and turned the corner.

In the next aisle, Chris noticed a book that looked interesting and reached to remove it from the shelf. As he was doing this, he noticed a distinguished looking man sitting at a table in the middle of the aisle. Surprised to find he was not alone, Chris took another look. The man wore thick glasses, which stood out against his curly white hair and beard. Startled at seeing Chris, the man briefly looked up from his book but then buried his head in it again. As for Chris, he felt taken aback by the stranger's presence. He returned the book to its place on the shelf and walked towards the library's exit, ready to leave.

The librarian sitting near the door stopped Chris, as if sensing he was frustrated about something. "Did you find what you were looking for?" she asked pleasantly.

"No I didn't," said Chris.

"What was it you were interested in? Maybe I can help you," she said.

"I'm looking for something on endemic trees," Chris replied.

"Oh," said the librarian, "Can I make a suggestion. Why don't you start by going to the Botanical Gardens and reading the labels on the species you discover there. This would give you a clear idea and picture of what you're looking for. You can proceed from there."

This was just the advice both his parents had given but coming from the librarian made it seem all the more wise. So, off he went.

The next day was Sunday and Chris, the twins, and their parents went back to the Botanical Gardens together. The family spread a blanket under the canopy of a huge tree, which the label identified as a Banyan tree. The twins didn't sit for too long and were soon running up and down in their usual playful manner. Chris had brought his favorite bird kite with him so he took off to find a hill from which to launch it. Almost as soon as he reached the spot, he became distracted by the sound of birds chirping and chattering noisily. Looking over his shoulder, Chris discovered that the noise came from a pair of bluebirds perched on the branch of a nearby cedar tree. Then he did a double take, for to his surprise the same stranger he had seen in the library was walking towards a bird box situated atop a long pole. Moving closer to the box, the man reached into it and pulled out a nest. Chris was surprised to see that the man then destroyed the nest. While he watched in dismay, Chris was distracted by a voice behind him. It was his father. When Chris turned back to look at the bird box, the man had gone. He had vanished just as quickly as he had appeared.

CHAPTER FOUR

The Spectacle

Monday was the last day of school before spring break. Chris could not wait for classes to end. He wished he could close his eyes and open them again to find the school day had ended. However, when he arrived at his math class he discovered that Mr. Gray had prepared a quiz for everyone. Placing the questions on each student's desk, the teacher informed the class that it had a half hour to complete the test. Looking at his watch, Mr. Gray then instructed the class to begin. After that, he would interrupt the silence every ten minutes to say how much time was left.

Ten minutes before it was time to hand in the papers Mr. Gray excused himself and said he would be back shortly. He had no sooner left the room than Tommy and Harry began throwing rolled pieces of paper around the room. Every time Chris got halfway through a problem, a missal would hit him, breaking his concentration. Then he had to start all over again. In frustration he shouted "Stop it!"

Of course that happened to be the very moment that Mr. Gray stepped back into the room. The math teacher looked angry. "I can't leave you for ten minutes without you making a spectacle of yourself. Go stand in the corner and show your fellow students trying to work some respect," he fumed. Then he turned to the class and said, "Time's up. Hand in your papers." Then the bell rang for recess. Everyone left the room except Chris.

Mr. Gray walked over to Chris, waving his test in the air at the same time. "What is this?" he asked. Before Chris could answer, he said "It seems to me that you make no effort at all. I expect more of you since you're the oldest in the class." Chris tried to speak but Mr. Gray continued, "Don't say a word. I want you to write a hundred times 'I will not make a spectacle of myself.'"

"Yes sir," said Chris meekly. A day that he had been longing to end was turning out to be the longest school day of his life. When it finally ended, Chris took several deep breaths and let out a sigh of relief.

When Chris arrived home, he was comforted to find his mother outside the cottage. She was busy weeding in the garden, assisted by the twins, who were covered in mud. Excited to see him, the girls ran over and pounced on him, hugging him with their muddy arms and hands. Chris didn't mind. He was just happy to be home. That was until his mother interrupted the play to announce that his father wished to see him inside.

Separating himself from the twins, Chris went into the house. His father was sitting in the living room pretending to read the newspaper. "You wanted to see me?" Chris asked.

"Yes," his father replied sternly. "Take a seat and tell me how your day at school went."

"It was fine," Chris said. His father smiled at that.

"Son, I'm going to get right to the point. Your mother and I had to visit the principal today. She suggested that it might be in your best interest if you were in a special school."

Chris's eyes widened and he blurted out, "Is that because I'm not as smart as the other kids?"

"No," said his father. "It's because you learn differently from them." Chris drew in his breath. "Don't worry," said his father. "I told the principal that you are making an effort and that soon she'll notice improvement."

At that Chris smiled, "Is that all then?"

"Yes son," his father said.

Chris went to his room to change out of his school clothes. Encouraged by his father's support, he decided he would go to the Botanical Gardens to look for some more endemic plants. He began to look for his notepad but after searching high and low couldn't find it anywhere. Finally, he went outside to ask his mother if she had seen it. She said no so he asked the twins, who seemed to have settled down. They began walking around the cottage towards the porch. There, sitting on the table, was his pad. He could see that every page was torn.

Chris shouted angrily at the twins and then stormed off to the path that led to the Botanical Gardens. When he reached the Garden, he sat down on the nearest bench, barely aware of his surroundings. Instead of noticing the lush vegetation all around him, he was thinking about all the things that had gone wrong on this day. Feeling as though nothing was going his way, Chris began to cry. Through his tears he noticed a man dressed completely in white, right up to the safari hat on his head, carrying a small pot containing a plant in one hand and a garden shovel in the other. As Chris continued to look, the man knelt down and began to dig a hole with the shovel.

The man in white removed the plant from its pot, pushed it into the hole and then firmly pressed the soil back around it. The man looked pleased with his work. Putting his hands on his hip, he looked up at the sky. Suddenly aware of another presence, he turned and noticed Chris. For a split second, Chris and the stranger locked eyes. Chris couldn't believe it. It was the same person he had seen in the library and then in the Gardens destroying the bird's nest. Chris looked again but by then the stranger had vanished.

Chris walked over to the spot where the unknown man had been digging. He read the label and noted that the plant was a Bermuda cedar. Chris smiled, inhaled and then exhaled. He felt very calm. He couldn't wait to go home and apologize to Carol and Sara for shouting at them. Running as fast as he could, he reached home to find his family about to start dinner. The twins looked nervous when they saw him. They were still feeling hurt about what Chris had said to them. Chris apologized, hugged them and told them that he loved them. It was an emotional moment for his mother and tears welled in her eyes. Chris went over and hugged her too. His father looked on and smiled before saying, "It looks as though someone is maturing into a fine young man."

BERMUDA
BERMUDA CEDAR

CHAPTER FIVE

Nonsuch Island

"Chris, Chris," a voice echoed in Chris's ear. It was his mother waking him from a deep sleep. "It's time to get up," she said. Chris groaned, stretched his legs then curled up into a ball and pulled the covers over his head. Soon he felt someone pulling them off again. It was Sara who then ran out of the room screaming "Chris is up!"

During breakfast, Mrs. Watson told the children to hurry up and eat because they were in for a surprise. After they had finished breakfast, Mrs. Watson made sandwiches and drinks, which she packed neatly into a basket. She then directed everyone towards the car. Sara held up the procession by crying for her doll. Mrs. Watson told Chris to run back and get it. "Hurry up," she said as he trotted off.

Chris soon returned with a doll in his left hand and his right hand hidden behind his back. Seeing her sister's doll, Carol began to cry for her own doll. Chris quickly pulled his right hand out from behind his back and held up the second doll. His father nodded approvingly. "Good work," he said. "I'm glad to see you thinking ahead." Chris smiled, feeling proud.

In the car, Chris sat silently with a satisfied look on his face as they drove towards the east end of the island. At their destination, Mr. Watson parked the car and they all got out and began walking towards a nearby dock, where a boat was tied up. They were greeted by its captain, a tall man with a bushy, curly mustache. "Hi folks," he called. "I'm Mr. Rego, your skipper. This is my assistant, Joel," he added, pointing to a smaller man with a round, happy face and big smile. Mr. Rego started the engine while Joel untied the ropes that held the boat to the dock. As they gained speed and headed towards an island visible in the distance, Mrs. Watson tightly held onto the girls, who screamed the whole way.

After a while, Mr. Rego turned off the engine and Joel dropped the anchor. "This is as far as we go," the skipper announced. Just then Chris noticed a smaller boat approaching them. He could see that the man driving it was wearing a safari hat, just like the stranger in the library and Botanical Gardens. Embarrassed, Chris put his head down to avoid eye contact. Mr. Rego introduced the newcomer as the Government Conservation Officer.

One by one Joel helped the Watsons onto the other boat. Chris was the last to go onboard and, wishing to appear independent, he refused Joel's help. Instead, he tried to jump onto the other boat by himself. He lost his footing and would have fallen overboard if the Conservation Officer hadn't grabbed him. It was then that Chris noticed that this wasn't the stranger he had seen before. Instead of a white beard this man was clean shaven and the hair poking out from under his safari hat was black. This man was much younger than the man he had seen in the library. Chris thought about this as they settled into the new boat and made their progress towards an island directly in front of them.

As they drew closer to the island, Chris noticed a sign that read Nonsuch Island. He couldn't believe his eyes. "Chris," his mother said, "there's nothing like experiencing the real thing firsthand, so here we are!"

The Conservation Officer tied up the boat and, after they were all off it, he gathered everyone around him. "It's important that we keep together," he said. "There are several paths and it's easy to get lost." Continuing, he said, "I'm Mr. Madeiros, the warden and caretaker of Nonsuch Island as well as all the other nature reserves throughout Bermuda."

Mr. Madeiros went on to explain that he was the successor of Dr. David Wingate, who had retired as Conservation Officer a few years back. Mr. Madeiros explained how in 1951 Dr. Wingate had been part of a team that rediscovered the Cahow, a bird thought to be extinct already by the early 1600s. At the time, Dr. Wingate was only fifteen years old and working on a school science project. Mr. Madeiros looked at Chris and said, "He wouldn't have been much older than you." He explained how in 1951 there were only eighteen pairs of Cahows world-wide but that in the forty-five years since then the number had grown to eighty-five pairs.

Looking around while the conservation officer was speaking, Mr. Watson noticed an old, partially submerged shipwreck. Pointing to it, he asked, "What is that sticking up out of the water over there?"

"That's a ship," Mr. Madeiros replied. "It was sunk deliberately in 1930 by Dr. William Beebe, a scientist who had specialized in coral reef research and in deep sea diving. He wanted it to be an artificial reef that would provide boats with shelter from strong winds."

"That name rings a bell," Chris's mother interjected.

"It should," replied Mr. Madeiros. "He's pretty famous. If you've been to the Bermuda Underwater Exploration Institute you would have seen a huge blue ball that he used to go down to the depths of the ocean. Dr. Beebe dove down to 3,028 feet in it. Before that, the deepest the divers could go was 400 feet."

"That's amazing!" exclaimed Mr. Watson.

"That's not all," said Mr. Madeiros. "Dr. Beebe also named lots of the fish you see swimming around Bermuda, including the Bream, which is endemic to the island." Hearing that word Chris's ears perked up and a light bulb went off in his mind.

Moving on, the warden led them up some steps—forty according to Chris' count—to the main house, which looked like a postcard of bygone Bermuda. Trees framed either side of the cottage, forming a shady canopy around it. Birds were singing. "It's like a living museum," thought Chris. From the cottage there was a view of the ocean beyond, an endless stretch of blue that looked calm and peaceful. Chris's mother and the twins sat on the porch to enjoy the view. Chris and his father chose to continue the tour.

Mr. Madeiros gave a brief history of the cottage. It had been used as a hospital for the yellow fever outbreak of 1865 he informed them. "Why was that?" asked Mr. Watson. "Is it because it was apart from the mainland? And how did yellow fever arrive in Bermuda anyway? You'd think being an island it would be isolated from diseases."

"Yellow fever came here through mosquitoes, which arrived on the island in water stored on ships," Mr. Madeiros said. "When the ships docked, the hatches were opened and the mosquitoes escaped, infecting over five hundred people."

"How long were people kept isolated on Nonsuch Island," asked Chris.

"Nonsuch served as a quarantine station and hospital from 1865 until 1914, the year World War I broke out," replied Mr. Madeiros. "After that the station was relocated to Coney Island."

Changing the subject, Chris' father wanted to know how they managed to get electricity out to Nonsuch Island. "That question's easy to answer," said the warden. "Everything is solar powered. Well almost everything," he corrected himself. "We use a generator to run heavy equipment." Then, continuing the tour, he led Chris and his father to another building. "This is where professors and student researchers launch their study of coral reefs during the summer months."

By this time, Mr. Watson was thinking about the rest of the family back at the cottage, sitting on the porch. "Let's go find the others," he said. "They're probably thinking we've gotten lost." This proved a good idea, for when the explorers returned to the cottage they were greeted with the sandwiches and lemonade Mrs. Watson had so carefully packed before they left home.

While they were enjoying their lunch, Mrs. Watson noticed a tiny bird, no bigger than a human thumb. "That's a Chick-of-the-Village," said Mr. Madeiros. "It's endemic to Bermuda." Looking at Chris, he continued, "You know what that word means don't you?" Excited, Chris nodded his head. A light bulb went off again as he realized he was gathering more and more material for his science project.

Out of the blue, Sara began to sing. "One little pig, two little pigs," she chanted.

Mr. Madeiros said, "That reminds me of something. Do you know the legend about pigs in Bermuda's history?" Sara looked puzzled. "Well according to the story the first people to arrive in Bermuda were Portuguese. They didn't settle but left behind lots of pigs."

"Why in the world did they do that?" asked Mrs. Watson.

"There were several reasons," replied the warden in response to her perfectly reasonable question. "You know how bad the weather can get around Bermuda during the winter months? In the early years ships found it hard to navigate our reefs during storms and there were lots of shipwrecks. Sailors would have found little food available on the island once they came ashore. So, it is believed, the Portuguese left behind the pigs so that shipwrecked sailors would find food."

"As you probably know," Mr. Madeiros continued, "pigs squeal and can make quite a bit of noise. Sailors would hear them from far off and in those days, when people were more superstitious than they are today, the rumor spread that the island was haunted."

"The Cahows didn't help," Mr. Madeiros added. "They only come ashore to land at night. They glide at speeds up to fifty miles an hour—faster than our speed limit for cars— and make a lot of noise. In fact, their calls are quite eerie. So all in all you can see how the sailors' imagination got the better of them."

"OK folks," said Mr. Madeiros, "Right now we're on the leeward side of the island. The weather here is beautiful. However, the other side of the island can be a different story. It can get really windy. That's why it's called the windward side. It's open to the whole Atlantic Ocean. Anyway, if the wind is blowing thirty miles an hour over on the mainland, it's usually blowing fifty miles an hour out here on Nonsuch Island. We're going to stay on the eastern part of the island, which is calmer. We'll bypass the man-made swamp and follow the path that leads past the graveyard to one of the three beaches on the island."

As they walked towards the path, Mr. Madeiros stopped and pointed to a dark cloud hanging overhead. "If that cloud doesn't move away soon, I'm going to have to cancel this tour and get you folks back to the mainland. The weather out here can get really bad, and fast." He had no sooner finished his sentence when heavy raindrops began falling. As the drops turned into a steady downpour, the family, led by Mr. Madeiros, raced towards the boat where Mr. Rego and Joel were waiting to help them aboard. However, Mr. Watson held back a little and Chris noticed that he whispered something to Mr. Madeiros, who nodded his head.

Later that night when the twins were already asleep, exhausted from the day's outing, Mr. Watson came into the bedroom and asked Chris how he had enjoyed the day. "It was great!" said Chris. Then his father asked him if he would like to go out to Nonsuch again. Chris couldn't believe his ears. "You bet I would," he exclaimed. Smiling, his father told him that his wish would be granted because he had told Mr. Madeiros about the science project and the conservationist had offered to let Chris tag along with him for a few days. Hearing this Chris shouted with delight and almost jumped out of his bunk.

"Here," said Mr. Watson, handing Chris a rather large paper bag. "You might need what's inside. And by the way, go to sleep. You're going to be getting up early tomorrow."

After his father left the room, Chris opened the bag and took a peek inside. A smile lit up his face when he discovered its contents. Inside the bag was a camera, a writing pad, several pencils and a pencil sharpener. Chris let out a big, happy sigh. Then he lay back on his bed and went to sleep.

CHAPTER SIX

Bermuda's National Bird

Bright and early the next day, Chris and his father drove down to a cove in Tucker's Town where they found Mr. Madeiros waiting for them on the same boat they had been on the day before. Next to it was a similar, more beaten-up boat, which had the words "*Rare Bird*" painted on its side. After saying goodbye to his father, Chris and Mr. Madeiros left for Nonsuch Island. As their boat made its way out into Castle Harbour, Mr. Madeiros pointed out Castle Island, telling Chris that all the islands to the west of Nonsuch were accessible to the public. Chris asked about the size of Nonsuch and Mr. Madeiros told him it was fifteen acres.

From the boat, Nonsuch looked even more beautiful to Chris than it had the day before. "It will look even better as time goes on," Mr. Madeiros informed him. Steering the boat around the sunken shipwreck, he added, "Gradually endemic plantings will replace the introduced ones like casuarinas, which are fast-growing trees that were planted to shelter the young endemics from the strong winds. When the endemics are tall enough, the casuarinas will be taken out."

When the pair finally reached Nonsuch, Mr. Madeiros tied up the boat and they disembarked. They trudged up the forty steps and made their way to the path that led to the western side of the island. This part of the island was very open and the wind was so strong that Chris' voice whistled as he exclaimed, "It's like going into a different zone."

"Yes, it's very different from the eastern side of the island," Mr. Madeiros agreed. At the same time, he stooped down to inspect a nest burrowed into the ground some yards back from the cliff face. He told Chris it was a man-made nest in which, hopefully, the Cahow would nest.

Then Mr. Madeiros told Chris all about the Cahow. Chris listened intently as the conservationist explained that the Cahow doesn't nest for three years. He told Chris how in the first year the male will visit the nest; then in the second year will try and attract a female to it. Finally, in the third year the female will lay one egg. "That's amazing!" declared Chris. "No wonder they almost became extinct!"

"If you think that's amazing," Mr. Madeiros replied, "Think about this. The Cahow mother flies about five hundred miles out to sea to find food for her chicks."

"Wow!" said Chris. "That's almost to the States."

"That's right," said Mr. Madeiros, "sometimes she leaves the new born chick alone for two or three days between feedings. In the meantime the baby Cahow survives on its fat."

"Really," said Chris. "How can the mother Cahow fly five hundred miles out and five hundred miles back without sleeping? That's a thousand miles."

"The Cahow spends most of its life flying," replied Mr. Madeiros. "In fact, it only lands to feed its chicks. The rest of the time it is flying. The Cahow can also drink salt water because of a gland in its beak that filters out salt. Furthermore, it can even sleep and fly at the same time. The Cahow glides through the air with one part of its brain shut down. If it happens to go near something, the sleeping part of the brain wakes up."

Chris was fascinated. "Well who looks after the babies?"

"The chicks are fed by their parents at night. Otherwise they scout the island by themselves. When they are big enough, they leave the island and never land again until they are ready to nest and have chicks of their own." As he was saying this, Mr. Madeiros bent down and removed something from the entrance to the man-made nest. "This is a baffle," he said. "It's a partition that will allow only a Cahow to fit through."

"Why would you need that?" Chris asked.

"Well," said Mr. Madeiros, "the Longtail flies around out here too. In fact, it competes with the Cahow for nests. If the Longtail were to get into a Cahow's nest it would scare the chicks away and take over the nest. Since the Longtail is larger than the Cahow, a baffle can prevent this by letting only the smaller Cahow into the nest."

Chris knelt down to take a closer look at the baffle. He noticed it had a small oval hole similar to the shape of a Cahow's body. "Since the Longtail's body is round, it would be like trying to push a square through a circle," Mr. Madeiros explained. At that he lay right down on the ground and looked over the edge of the cliff. "I'm looking to see if there is any sign the Longtails are nesting early."

Looking back at Chris, Mr. Madeiros said, "By the way, the Longtail is not Bermuda's national bird. The Cahow is. Chris smiled at that. He couldn't wait to pass that bit of information on to his father who had told him that the Longtail was Bermuda's national bird. Mr. Madeiros smiled and, as if he were reading Chris's mind, said, "The Longtails are tropical birds which start to nest in April. There are over six hundred of their nests lodged in the cliffs around Bermuda. This is the biggest concentration in the northern hemisphere." With that Mr. Madeiros looked at his watch and said he had to go back to the mainland. He explained that he had a meeting with Government, which was in the process of making Cooper's Island to the east a public attraction.

Chris decided it was time to take some pictures, so he fished out his camera and began to snap.

CHAPTER SEVEN

Dr. Wingate

On day two of his visit to Nonsuch, Chris helped Mr. Madeiros pull up casuarinas from around the many cedar trees planted on the island. "Casuarinas are very fast growing," Mr. Madeiros explained. "We don't want them taking over. They were only planted to protect the cedars from the wind as they establish themselves."

"Why are cedar trees so important?" asked Chris.

"They have been important from Bermuda's earliest days," replied Mr. Madeiros. "The early settlers used them to build houses, furniture and boats. In fact all of Bermuda's endemics were a salvation to the first settlers. Every part of the palmetto was put to use. The leaves made thatch roofs, the berries were eaten and the bark was ground up to make flour." Then the conservationist looked at his watch and said, "Let's check out the eastern side of the island before it gets too late."

Chris followed Mr. Madeiros along the path leading to the man-made swamp. Endemic olivewood trees formed a dense canopy over their heads. As they neared the swamp, they spied a heron standing as still as a statue in the middle of it. Pointing at the graceful bird, Mr. Madeiros identified it as a Yellow Crown Night Heron, a species introduced to replace a heron that had lived in Bermuda years ago. Continuing on their way, the two passed the graveyard for yellow fever victims. About fifty yards beyond the graveyard, the path widened to expose a beach with beautiful pink sand. The view was spectacular and the pair sat down on the rocks next to the beach to take it all in.

"Forty years ago, we placed 16,000 Green Turtle eggs on this beach. Little did we know back then that it takes over forty years for a turtle to mature," said Mr. Madeiros, shaking his head.

"That's a long time," said Chris.

"That's not all," said Mr. Madeiros. "The sex of turtles is determined by climate. Not too long ago scientists discovered that the majority of turtles born in tropical climates are female whereas those born in semi-tropical climates like Bermuda are mostly males. So what we now have in Bermuda is a lot of lonely male turtles swimming around."

Suddenly Chris noticed a slimy creature poised on the rocks, right next to him. Startled, he jumped. "What's that thing?" he cried.

Mr. Madeiros laughed and said, "It's just a skink."

"What's a skink?" Chris asked.

"It's a type of lizard that's endemic to Bermuda," Mr. Madeiros replied as he placed a finger on the creature and gently rubbed its back. Surprisingly, the skink did not move. "Touch it yourself. It won't hurt you," instructed Mr. Madeiros.

Chris reached out and gingerly touched the skink's back. "It feels like a fish that's been taken out of the water," he said.

Time seemed to fly and all too soon it was time to return to the boat. As they made their way back to the mainland, Chris mused to himself about how much he had learned in such a short time. As they passed the ship that had been sunk to protect smaller boats from the rough sea, he looked up and noticed a boat headed in their direction. As it got closer, Chris noticed something written on the side of the boat. Squinting, he picked out the words "*Rare Bird*." The boat pulled alongside them and its driver turned off the engine. Mr. Madeiros said good day to him. "Who's your passenger?" the newcomer asked.

Chris looked at the *Rare Bird* and its occupant and then looked again. He couldn't believe his eyes. It was the same man he had seen destroying a bluebird nest in the Botanical Gardens. He looked away when Mr. Madeiros tried to introduce him but the stranger put out his hand and said, "I'm Dr. David Wingate. I'm pleased to meet you."

On the way back to the mainland, Chris was silent. Noticing this, Mr. Madeiros asked him if he was alright. Chris hesitated before saying, "I always thought Dr. Wingate loved birds."

"Why of course he does," replied Mr. Madeiros. "What would make you think otherwise?"

Chris hesitated before saying, “Well I once saw him destroy a nest in a bluebird box.”

“Oh,” laughed Mr. Madeiros. “Bluebird boxes are only for bluebirds but sometimes sparrows invade them and make nests in them. Dr. Wingate was only removing a sparrow’s nest. He could tell it was a sparrow’s nest because sparrows use anything to make their messy nests, whereas bluebirds make very neat and clean nests.”

By this time they had reached their destination. Chris thanked Mr. Madeiros for taking the time to help him with his science project. Mr. Madeiros told Chris that if he worked hard he too could become a conservation officer one day. That evening, Chris repeated this to his father, who was happy to see the excitement in his son’s eyes as he related all the things he had learned out on Nonsuch Island.

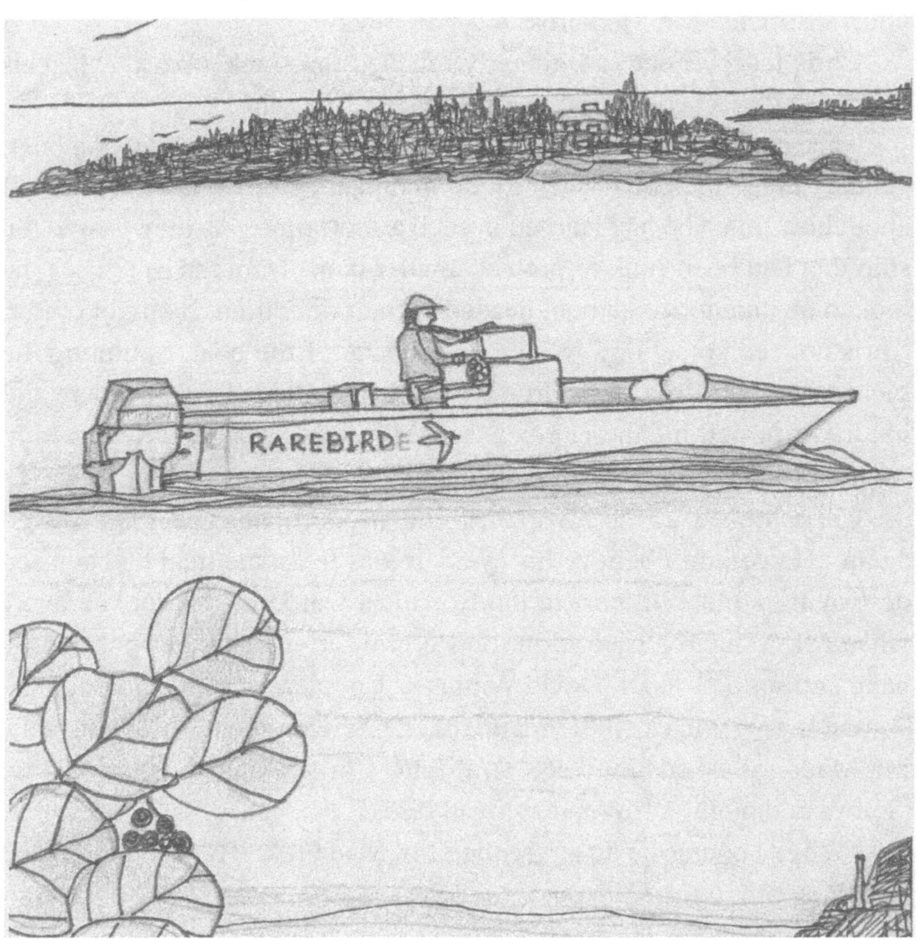

CHAPTER EIGHT

All Subjects Are Important

Early Monday morning Chris woke up to a voice echoing throughout his room. It was like a ball bouncing off the walls. It was his mother calling, "Chris, Chris. Get up or you'll be late for school."

Heeding that familiar refrain, Chris got up, ate his breakfast and ran out the door, shouting goodbye over his shoulder to the twins. But as he neared the bus stop, Chris could see the rear of the bus moving away from him. He shouted to get the driver's attention but all his cries were in vain. The driver did not hear him and kept on going. Chris shifted his backpack, straightened his shoulders and started walking.

When Chris finally reached school, about an hour after he had set out, class had already started. As he entered the classroom, Mrs. Burt looked straight at him and, in a loud, accusing voice, said, "You're late." Chris tried to explain but she was not interested. "Missing the bus is no excuse," she said. Then, turning back to the class, she announced that today's class would be spent preparing for Friday's exam. "Arrange yourselves into pairs to study," she instructed.

Chris took a seat by himself at the back of the class. It seemed that no one wanted to be his study partner. He even felt that the other kids were grinning and talking about him. He tried to block it all out and put his head down to concentrate on his work.

When the class was over and his classmates were gathering their things and walking out of the room, Mrs. Burt took Chris aside and asked him if his parents had talked to him about transferring to another school. Chris told her that he was working hard to improve and that his father was helping him. "Do you call coming to class late improving?"

demanded Mrs. Burt. Chris apologized again. "Sorry, has nothing to do with it. There are special schools for children like you," she said. "I don't mean that in a bad way. I'm just trying to help you Chris. I think you're father should get another professional opinion." Then, as if she had just been talking about the weather, Mrs. Burt dismissed him. "That'll be all, you can go now." Her words echoed in Chris's mind for the rest of the school day. He could think of nothing else.

When Chris arrived home at the end of the school day, he did his best to hide his emotions. He hugged his mother as usual and went outside to spend some time playing with his twin sisters. Later he told his mother he was going to the Botanical Gardens to study. When he reached the Gardens, Chris sat down on a bench to settle his emotions. Then he opened his math book to study, but try as he might he could not make himself interested in this subject. Finally he put the book down and began staring ahead blankly. All he could think about was how he was going to fail his exam and fulfill the low expectations of Mrs. Burt and his classmates. Chris was feeling pretty depressed and sorry for himself when he was startled by a hand on his shoulder. He looked up. To his surprise, there was Dr. Wingate, who seemed to recognize him.

"Mr. Madeiros told me about your science project," the conservationist said, picking up the math book Chris had just put down. Looking it over, he said. "Good move. I wish that when I was your age I had realized how every subject is important and connected to whatever career you choose later in life."

"How is that?" Chris asked suspiciously.

Dr. Wingate sat down beside him and, looking over the top of his glasses, said, "When I was a young boy, school was not my cup of tea. I tried every excuse I thought my parents would believe to get out of going." Then he scratched his head, took off his glasses and said, "I was failing every class. My teachers had given up on me. They even suggested that my parents put me in another school." Chris couldn't believe his ears. It was as if Dr. Wingate was describing his own life. Dr. Wingate continued, "Then one day my whole outlook on life changed." Chris perked up his ears on hearing these words. Dr. Wingate went on with his story.

"It was early November," he reminisced. "My father and I were sitting on the porch waiting for the first star to appear." Dr. Wingate turned to Chris and told him how his father had always talked to him about the heavens and the stars. Then he related how on one particular evening, just after the sun had set and birds were twittering in the trees, his father told him about another bird, a bird of the night called the Cahow.

Sitting up straight, the conservationist said, "I became excited. I wondered if this bird, which my father said no longer existed, was really extinct. I wondered if by some chance it might still be found in some remote, undeveloped part of Bermuda. I became preoccupied with the idea that it might still exist in someplace like the islands in Castle Harbour."

Dr. Wingate then put his glasses back on. "I knew then what I wanted to be; I wanted to become a conservation officer. I also knew that to achieve that I would need an education. That would mean studying and passing math, English and all the other subjects."

Chris sat quietly. He was taking in everything Dr. Wingate said. A smile formed on his face as he made up his mind that he would follow Dr. Wingate's advice, and also his path in life. As if recognizing that smile, the conservationist stood up and said, "I'd better be going. Good luck on your exams."

Later that evening, with Dr. Wingate's words still echoing in his ears, Chris opened the dreaded math and English textbooks. He realized now how important all his subjects were if he wanted to fulfill his new dream of becoming a conservation officer one day.

CHAPTER NINE

The Final Exam

The rest of the week flew by and, before Chris knew it, Friday had arrived and he and his classmates were seated in a large room waiting for Mrs. Burt to hand out the exam. She put a copy of the test on each student's desk and announced that there would be five exams given throughout the day with a half-hour break between each one. "Do your best and good luck," she said by way of offering encouragement.

The math exam came first. Chris looked over all the questions and decided to do the easiest ones first. In what seemed no time at all to Chris, he noticed Mrs. Burt looking at her watch. "You have fifteen minutes left," she announced. Chris looked around and noticed that all his classmates had put down their pencils and appeared ready to dash out of the room as soon as the time was up. He decided to spend the remaining time looking over his answers.

"Time's up," Mrs. Burt declared as she walked over to Chris and stretched out her hand. "Give me your paper please." She had to repeat herself before Chris heard her. Afterwards, when the other students were enjoying their break, Chris spent the time preparing for the next exam.

It was a long and draining day for everyone. The science project was the final test of the day. The strain of the long day was becoming evident, for sighs could be heard throughout the room. More than once Mrs. Burt had to call for silence. Finally, it was all over and she collected the papers, telling the class she would have the results for them on Monday.

When Chris arrived home, the smell of an apple pie baking in the oven greeted him even before he reached the door. Later that evening, the family sat out on the porch to enjoy it. It was a beautiful, clear night. The sky was lit up by thousands of stars. After they had finished the desert, Mrs. Watson escorted the twins into the house to get ready for bed. Left behind, Chris and his father sat quietly for a while, enjoying the peace. Chris' father broke the silence to ask how the budding conservation officer had done on his exams that day. Chris told him he had tried his best but some of the questions had been difficult. His father reassured him, telling him it was alright as long as he had tried.

Saturday turned out to be a fun day for everyone. The family went to the Aquarium, where the twins were very taken with the monkeys and the way they swung from branch to branch, entertaining their audience. Carol couldn't resist sticking her hand into the cage. Luckily, Mr. Watson saw her and pulled her hand back just as a monkey was about to grab it. The lighthearted mood continued on the car ride back home as the twins sang one favourite song after another.

The next day was Sunday and Chris awoke to the aroma of bacon streaming into his room from the kitchen, where his mother was preparing breakfast. During breakfast the phone rang and his mother went to pick it up. Later, after breakfast, Chris noticed his mother take his father aside into the living room. Chris went back to his room and was busy cleaning it when his father came in and closed the door behind him. He looked hard at Chris, a certain look in his eyes. Chris knew that stare. He had seen it many times, mostly when he had done something wrong. "Take a seat, Chris," his father said sternly. "Your mother has received a phone call from Mrs. Davis, the school principal. She wants to see us first thing tomorrow morning, before classes start. Son, is there anything you want to tell me?"

Chris thought before replying and then said, "Dad, I can't think of anything. I've done nothing wrong."

Mr. Watson looked Chris straight in the eye and said, "Are you absolutely sure about that? Something must be wrong for the principal to call on a Sunday morning." As his father walked out of the room, Chris began to wonder what he could possibly have done wrong. All he could imagine was that he had completely failed his exams and the principal was about to tell him it was time to make arrangements to transfer somewhere else.

On Monday morning, Chris and his parents arrived at school early. While they waited outside the principal's office, Chris grew more and more anxious, especially as he felt other students were pointing in his direction and smiling knowingly. Finally the secretary announced that the principal was ready to see them. They all filed into her office, Chris following closely in his parents footsteps. Mrs. Davis and Mrs. Burt were standing side by side. The principal pointed to some chairs and invited them to sit down. She then apologized for calling them at home on a Sunday morning. Continuing, she said, "I think you'll find it was worth it though when you find out why I called."

Mrs. Burt spoke first. "As you know," she began, "I have been recommending that Chris find another school, one more suited to his needs." She hesitated for what seemed an eternity to Chris, who looked at his mother. Mrs. Watson was slumped in her chair. Noticing this, Mrs. Burt continued, saying, "I want to be the first to say I was wrong about your son, he not only passed his exams but in at least one he also excelled, topping the rest of the class by far." Startled, Mrs. Watson sat up and looked at the teacher, as if she was not quite sure what she was hearing. Mrs. Burt repeated what she had told them and said, "I am so sorry for being so quick to judge."

Mrs. Davis then interrupted saying, "Your son's science exam was not only the best in the class, it was one of the best I have seen in twenty years." Then she walked over to the door and opened it. To Chris's great surprise, there stood Mr. Madeiros.

"Hi, again," waved Mr. Madeiros. "I'll bet you can't guess why I'm here. As you know," he continued, "Government holds a summer camp out on Nonsuch each year. Based on your enthusiasm and results, they've agreed to have you come out and act as my assistant next summer. There's a lot you can do to help me and you'll learn something too."

Chris couldn't believe it. He was almost speechless but somehow managed to say "Thank you. Thank you." Smiling, Chris remembered his father's advice, "If you move slowly, you have to move early." How true, how true, he thought to himself.

The End

Did You Know?

Dragonflies eat Ticks
Lizards eat Fruitflies
Herons eat Crabs and Frogs.
Kiskadees eat Lizards.
Ladybugs Eat Aphids and Scale Insects.
Frogs eat Cockroches, Centipedes, Ants, Flies, Aphids and Woodlice.

There is a Bee that only lives on Castle Harbour Islands.
Called the Solitary Bee,
it is twice the size of our Honey Bee.

Bermuda Has Seventeen Endemic Plants

1. Bermuda Sedge
2. Bermuda Spike Rush
3. Bermudiana
4. Bermuda Bay Bean
5. Bermuda Campylopus
6. Bermuda Trichostomum
7. Bermuda Shield Fern
8. Governor Laffan's Fern
9. Bermuda Maidenhair Fern
10. Bermuda Cave Fern
11. Bermuda Cedar
12. Bermuda Palmetto
13. Bermuda Olivewood
14. Bermuda Snowberry
15. Wild Bermuda Pepper
16. Darrell's Fleabane
17. St Andrew's Cross

There are two birds endemic to Bermuda
White Eye Viro or Chick of The Village
and The Bermuda Petrel or Cahow

The Skink is the only endemic Lizard in Bermuda

www.ingramcontent.com/pod-product-compliance
Lightning Source LLC
LaVergne TN
LVHW010108110826
845155LV00028B/550

* 9 7 8 1 9 2 6 6 0 9 0 1 0 *